52 Communion Meditations

Compiled by Andy Rector

STANDARD PUBLISHING
Cincinnati, Ohio

Library of Congress Cataloging in Publication Data:

52 communion meditations / compiled by Andy Rector
    p. cm.
    Includes index.
    ISBN 0-87403-830-8
    1. Lord's Supper—Prayer-books and devotions—English.
I. Rector, Andy. 2. Title: Fifty two communion meditations.
BV199.C6A14 1991
264'.13—dc20

Foreword

How are the Communion meditations at your church? There are at least five things necessary to make a good Communion meditation:

1. Prepared With Passion—A good preacher will spend many hours developing his sermon for Sunday. The thoughtful teacher will likewise invest much time in preparing his or her lesson for the Bible-school hour. A song leader, if he is worth his salt, will give much thought to the selection of the songs that will be sung. Those who are presiding at the Lord's table must also give much thought, time, and effort to the remarks they will render on the Lord's Day.

2. Tempered by Time—There are two extremes that should be avoided here. One is to make the meditation too long. The other is to make it too brief. Preparation will keep the Communion talk from being a rambling, convoluted affair. It will also prevent it from ending before it has barely begun.

3. Steeped in Scripture—Stories and illustrations are fine but they should never replace Scripture at the Lord's table. Peter exhorts, "If anyone speaks, he should do it as one speaking the very words of God" (1

Peter 4:11, *New International Version*). *The very words of God!* How appropriate for the Lord's Supper. Be sure that the Communion meditation is grounded in Scripture.

4. Centered on Christ—A fourth facet of improving the meditation at the Lord's Supper is to be sure that it is centered on Jesus Christ. After all, Jesus did say, "This do in remembrance of Me" (1 Corinthians 11:24). Paul told the Corinthians that he had determined not to know anything among them except Jesus Christ and Him crucified (1 Corinthians 2:2). This should be our desire as well.

5. Delivered With Decorum—Finally the Communion meditation should be presented in the best manner possible. We expect stateliness in statesmen; we should expect dignity in those presiding at the Lord's table. Not stuffiness or dryness, mind you. But real dignity.

Those who preside at the table of our Lord have a tremendously solemn duty to fulfill. On every Sunday it is the last Lord's Supper for someone. *That makes it his last supper.*

Tell the story as a dying man to dying men.

—Victor Knowles
Carthage, Missouri

Contents

Communion
Meditations

Let Me Be Broken

Scripture Reading: Matthew 26:26

(Read Scripture.)

How often we hear at Communion, "Jesus took bread, gave thanks and broke it, and gave it to His disciples, saying, 'Take and eat; this is my body.'" We thank God for Jesus, broken for us, as the bread symbolizes.

This one who was broken is the same Jesus who earlier stood among hungry people and calmly and assuredly broke five loaves to feed five thousand people. We picture Him there, looking into Heaven, thanking God, breaking the bread, and giving it away to a hungry crowd. We see that miracle bread as beautiful, perfect loaves, for God created it. But its value was not in the beauty, rather in its brokenness. For it was broken bread that met the needs of the hungry.

When Jesus paid the ultimate sacrifice, He prayed, "Not as I will, but as you will." This was His final and complete giving of

7

himself to be broken for us. The loaf was costly, yet adequate to meet every spiritual hunger.

As we approach His table, what does He see in us? Are we beautiful, whole, unbroken loaves He yearns to share? Were we not created by God with adequate ingredients to meet the needs of the crowd? Yet our value is not in the beauty of the created, but in our submission to be broken.

Prayer

Father, thank You for creating the loaf, with all its potential. Thank You for Jesus, the Bread of Life, for He is our perfect example of total submission. Here are our bodies, our time, our talent . . . not as we will, but as You will. Shape us and break us, again and again, so we can be used to feed the spiritually hungry around us. May the added fruit of Your Spirit make our service sweet and nourishing in our world. Amen.

—Kathleen Noe
Lebanon, Missouri

Date Used: _____

Visualizing Calvary

Scripture Reading: Hebrews 12:2

Visualization or imagery—the seeing of pictures in our minds—is used by many people today to help them overcome anxieties and to cause them to see things in different ways. We not only then make pictures in our minds, we make them in color or in black and white. We can make pictures bright or dim, still or moving, a short time back or a long time ago.

This is one thing that the writer is telling us in Hebrews 12:2 (**read Scripture**). The writer is asking us to look back to Calvary and see Jesus on the cross as He shed His blood for us. The fruit of the vine reminds us of this. We can see His body which was broken for us. The broken bread reminds us of this.

As we think about or visualize these great events at Calvary, we must remind ourselves that all else is minor compared to the death of Jesus for us.

Let us close our eyes and visualize Calvary where we see God's love shown. There we see Jesus suffering, dying, and forgiving. And because God loved us while we were sinners, we gather as the redeemed. We must concentrate on Christ at the table so that we, like the Emmaus disciples, may recognize Him in the breaking of bread.

Prayer

Lord, give us a vision of the body and blood. We need enlightenment concerning that celebration which is central to our worship, the Communion of the Lord's Supper. Amen.

—Douglas Wilson
Rochelle, Illinois

Date Used: _____

Jesus' New Kingdom

Scripture Reading: Matthew 26:26-29

(Read Scripture.)

Jesus came to a troubled world. His religious world was enslaved by legalistic literalism, a set of rules perpetuated by scribes. His political world was ruled by Rome. The people exalted the practice of an eye for an eye and a tooth for a tooth.

To this world of turmoil and mediocre morals, Jesus came to fulfill prophecy. He came to establish a new order of higher principles and ethics He would call the kingdom of God.

In all times and in all places, Jesus raised standards from selfishness, corruption, and cruelty, to consideration, kindness, and love. Jesus gives to us this new order, this new kingdom

To make His precious gift, Jesus had to fulfill the law by suffering the cruelty of the cross. So that all peoples of all times would remember and rise to the higher order of life, Jesus left to us symbols of His broken body and His shed blood.

To us, the broken bread and wine of our Communion service offers a place in the new kingdom of God. To us, this service demands our turning from mediocre morals to the righteousness of Christ's new order, Christ's kingdom of God on earth!

Prayer

Everlasting Father, as we come to this table, we thank you for Jesus, and for the new kingdom of God that He brought to our world. As our minds flash back across the centuries, we again see Jesus.

Jesus said that He would be with us when only a few are gathered in His name. Just now, we know that He is with us in this holy Communion service, as surely as He led the multitudes in Galilee.

Forgive our sins, we pray, and help us to walk in the ways of Jesus. Make us worthy to be with Him in His new kingdom of God on earth.

In His Holy Name, we pray. Amen.

—Emery Stoops
Pacific Palisades, California

Date Used: _____

The New Passover

Scripture Reading: John 1:29

As our Lord observed this Passover with His disciples, He continued teaching them of the coming of His new covenant. As we read this, we realize that the disciples did not fully understand the meaning.

The Passover has great historic significance to the Jews. When they observed it, they remembered how their ancestors were in cruel bondage in Egypt. After a series of plagues on the Egyptians, the Lord sent a death angel over the land to slay the first-born in each household. The remedy, or salvation, for the Hebrew was for each household to take an unblemished lamb, slay it, apply the blood on the doorpost of the house, and eat the lamb along with unleavened bread. They prepared to leave Egypt and go to the promised land.

The new Passover, the Lord's Supper, can be compared in many ways to the original Passover. The human race is also in bondage, not to Egypt, but to sin and its penalty. A remedy, or salvation, had been provided—the perfect lamb, Jesus Christ. John the Baptist recognized Him (**read Scripture**).

The promise of eternal life is given to those who personally accept the remedy. This promise, like the sparing of the first-born many years ago, is not given to all. The promise of salvation was and is given only to those who believe, accept, and apply the shed blood of the Lamb.

Prayer

Heavenly Father, thank you for sending Your Son to take away the sins of the world. Just as the Hebrew people were slaves, we today are slaves to sin. Only Jesus, the unblemished Lamb, can provide the remedy to free us. We thank You for that. Amen.

—Lloyd Robertson
Worthington, Minnesota

Date Used: _____

An Act of Obedience

Scripture Reading: 2 John 6

(Read Scripture.)

When Jesus instituted the Lord's Supper He spoke at length concerning its importance. During this time He uttered six words that have perhaps been quoted more often than any of the others. These words were, "Do this in remembrance of me." It becomes an act of obedience for Christians to come together in observance of the Lord's Supper because of these words of Jesus. The act of obedience becomes an act of love when we care enough to remember our Lord in this manner.

We have all performed many acts of obedience. It started when we were children and were taught to obey our parents. We did this, even though sometimes it was unpleasant. There are times one obeys because he feels he has to, but when love enters the picture, the task becomes an act of love. When we truly love someone, it is a joy to please him.

The more we learn of Jesus the more we love Him. We may be divided over certain aspects of our "religion" but on this point we surely all agree: Jesus was filled with love and compassion for others—the rich and the poor, the lovable and the unlovable. He was willing to give so much and ask for so little in return. How could one not love Him?

Let us be thankful for the opportunity to perform this act of obedience. For when it is done in His mercy, it becomes an act of genuine Christian love.

Prayer

Lord, help us to obey those six words Your Son uttered long ago: "Do this in remembrance of me." Help us to obey these words, not out of habit, but out of love. Because Your Son loved us, we love You, Lord, and now we show our love by observing the symbols of Your Son's body and blood. We remember Him. Amen.

—Leo C. Bennett
Windsor, Illinois

Date Used: _____

16

Complete in Christ

Scripture Reading: Matthew 26:26-28

(Read Scripture.)

In these verses Jesus says, "Take and eat, this *is* my body," and "This *is* my blood of the covenant, which is poured out for many for the forgiveness of sins" (New International Version, italics added). He used the present tense in referring to the physical elements that would make up the spiritual Lord's Supper. At the Communion table, partaking of the bread and the fruit of the vine, we come face to face with the relationship between the physical and the spiritual aspects of our own lives.

Present-day culture is so very physical in all aspects that we often fail to consider that God made us spiritual entities as well as physical beings. It is our spiritual nature that is involved when we refer to our creation in the image of God. A balance between our physical and spiritual natures is necessary if we are to fulfill God's purpose for our lives.

The above words of Jesus are spoken again in 1 Corinthians 11:24-26 by the apostle Paul, who tells of the purpose of the Communion service. As we participate in the table of memories given to us by our Lord and Savior, let us also include the fact that we are spiritual. We need the spiritual "food" that only the Word of God can give to us.

Prayer

Holy and loving Heavenly Father, we are grateful that You have provided the spiritual food that we need through Your Son and our Savior, Jesus Christ. We are thankful that He established this table of memories for us so that we can remember His great sacrifice for us and that we too can receive strength for our spirits. We pray for daily growth in our spiritual understanding through the help of the Holy Spirit. We thank You for these blessings. In the name of our blessed Savior, Jesus, Amen.

—Charles L. Wakelee
Seattle, Washington

Date Used: _____

Eating With Sinners

Scripture Reading: Matthew 9:11,12

(Read Scripture.)

This Scripture refers to the time just after Jesus had chosen Matthew as one of His apostles. He was hardly one of the religious leaders of the day, for Matthew was a tax collector. Men didn't have many good adjectives to use for those in his vocation.

The event that preceded this Scripture was a dinner. Matthew prepared a dinner and invited his cronies, a motley crowd of outcasts like himself. He invited them . . . and Jesus. Surely he wished to introduce his friends to the One who had brought meaning and purpose into his life. At any rate, the guest soon became the host, and the supper became His supper. Then the Pharisees asked His disciples why their teacher ate with publicans and sinners. Jesus gave the answer which is the heart of the gospel. He said that those who were well had no need of a physician, but those who were sick.

Today we come to another Supper—the Lord's Supper. And the question could well be asked again, and the same answer would apply. Critics of the church often point to our failures and shortcomings.

Sometimes we are too embarrassed to reply, knowing full well that they are true. But Christ answers for us. Why does the Master eat with sinners? It is a relevant question. Have not we, like Matthew, cheated God and been less than He planned for us to be? His Supper, however, is for sinners only. It is for sinners like us—those called out of the failures and broken promises of yesterday, sinners whom God has promised to remake into what we ought to be.

Here in this supper, we may welcome our Lord, pledge our faith, and join His friends. We find that we do not so much welcome Him as He welcomes *us*. He is the host who invites us to share in His body, broken for us, and His blood, shed so freely. How fortunate that He invites sinners to dinner!

Prayer

Father, thank You for inviting us to Your table. How wonderful that we are welcome not *despite* the fact that You know all there is to know about us, but because You know how much we need Your grace.In the name of the host, our Lord Jesus, Amen.

—Gary W. McKinney
Morton, Illinois

Date Used: _____

Union With Christ

Scripture Reading: 1 Corinthians 10:14-22

(Read Scripture.)

As Christians, we are called to leave behind the ways of the world. This passage both challenges and charges the Christian to seek only the ways of God. So often the Christian tries to blend the ways of the world with the Christian life; yet, the two cannot be mixed without compromise. They will not blend together smoothly.

The Gospel writers make it clear that a person cannot serve two masters. One need not look far to see the folly of those who would try to blend both the things of this world with the things of God. In such cases, the world takes over.

The apostle Paul understood how mankind loves the things of this world. He illustrates that our union with the Christ-event is a complete participation and union with Jesus in His death, burial, and resurrection. William Barclay illustrates the contrast between Christ and the world in this way:

One of the great statues of Christ is that by Thorwaldsen: after he had carved it, he was offered a commission to carve a statue

*of Venus for the Lourve. His answer was:
"The hand that carved the form of Christ can
never carve the form of a heathen goddess."*

Those who truly handle the things of Christ find it difficult to soil their hands with ungodly things. We are reminded of this fact as we are invited to gather around His table. We are invited by Christ to handle His blood and His body through this supper, to renew that union with Him in the event of His death and resurrection. We are called to separate ourselves from this world, seek forgiveness of sins and union with Christ at His table.

Prayer
God, You are our only Lord and Master. We know that we cannot serve both the world and Christ. Be with us, Father, when we are tempted to soil our hands with ungodly things. Help us to seek union with You. Thank You for the gathering around Your table. In Your Son's name we pray, Amen.

—Denney E. Edens
Elizabethton, Tennessee

Date Used: _____

Contacting the Lord

Scripture Reading: Galatians 2:20

The minds of men can never meet until they learn to communicate. The hearts and minds of mortals can never know God until they learn to commune with Him. At His table we can find real in-depth communion with the Lord.

In response to the command of the Lord himself—"This do in remembrance of me"—we assemble at the Lord's table on each Lord's Day. In this quiet moment in the week's rush and hurry, we can turn off the world. We can touch the eternal verities. Here we can get the priorities of life in proper focus.

According to Christ's own words (Matthew 26:26-28), the bread represents and commemorates the body of Christ given in sacrifice for our sins by Him who had no sin. The purpose is that His body, the church, might be free from sin.

The cup represents the shed blood of Christ for the remission of sins. As we partake of these emblems of life, we realize the enormity of the price the Lord paid for our sins and we renew our commitment to Him.

This is a sacred ordinance. We should approach in sincere repentance, deep humility, and heartfelt gratitude to Jesus for His sacrifice on Calvary's cross. We come to seek forgiveness for our failures. We also come to ask strength to overcome them.

In the Lord's Supper, as we partake in remembrance we are contacting the holy purity of the divine nature of our Lord, who in love that passes our understanding, loved us and gave himself for us (**read Scripture**).

Here, through the silent corridors of secret prayer we convey to our Lord our innermost yearnings to be all that He knows we should be. We repent. We must seek forgiveness for sin and strength to overcome evil temptations. Here we touch the spiritual care and concern of our God's love that gave us a Savior.

Prayer

Lord, in communing with You in mutual love, we are renewed and resolved to keep a closer walk with You, our Redeemer. Remind us of our great need for Your sustaining power to enable us to overcome sin and faithfully serve You in steadfast devotion.

—Stella Fain Hansford
Coweta, Oklahoma

Date Used: _____

Christ Is the Greatest

Scripture Reading: Luke 22:24

(Read Scripture.)

When Luke recorded the institution of the Lord's Supper, he gave us an insight not only into the divine life of Christ, but a look at the very human actions of the apostles also. This includes the final hours in the life of Christ preceding His mock trial and ultimate death on the cross.

Jesus told the apostles of the single most important event in the history of humanity, one that would ultimately change the world forever. He knew His death was imminent, but He continued to teach His apostles with all the love, patience, and understanding He had shown throughout His entire ministry.

Christ knew they did not fully understand what was about to happen or how it would affect their lives and change the world. Jesus had just spoken the words,

"This do in remembrance of me." Instead of having their minds on His words, the disciples began to argue among themselves about who was the greatest.

In reading Luke's words, we find a way to help heal us spiritually. We have to look beyond our own humanity to the words of Jesus, asking the Holy Spirit to guide us, not only as we partake of this feast of love, but on a daily basis. In doing this we look to the words of Christ and lose ourselves in them. We become one with Christ forever.

Prayer

Dear Father, we praise Your name and thank You for the life of Jesus Christ. In His death, He took our sins from us. In partaking of this loaf and cup, we remember they represent His broken body and shed blood. As we partake, may we each examine ourselves. Look to the very fiber of our souls and find us worthy in Your sight. Guide our lives with Your Holy Spirit that we may always do Your will instead of our own. In Jesus' name, Amen.

—Larry K. Eastham
Greenup, Kentucky

Date Used: _____

An Advocate

Scripture Reading: Job 16:19-22

(Read Scripture.)

Job knew what it meant to suffer, perhaps in ways that most of us could never know. His "friends" sought to minimize his pain, and to blame him for the trouble he was enduring. In Job, we see a picture of a man who loved God deeply, and yet realized how much every man differs from the Almighty Creator. Job knew that, if he were to understand God and His unsearchable ways, he would need someone to help him, an advocate before the Father. And, he knew as well that when his own life was over, and his journey into eternal life was begun, he would need a friend to "plead his case" before the righteous judge.

What a marvelous picture of grace at work which we see here in the Old Testament! We know that, as Christians, we do indeed have an advocate before the Father even our Lord Jesus Christ (1 John 2:1). He bore our sins on the tree, so that we can be presented blameless before God one day.

Each of us knows that one day we, too, must embark on that "journey of no return." As we pause to celebrate this time of communion with our Savior, let us be thankful that we do not have to take that journey alone. As our Redeemer and our friend, He goes with us every step of the way. Praise His name!

Prayer

Holy Father, You are our Almighty Creator. As Your created, we cannot understand Your ways; however, You have supplied us with an advocate. We know this advocate as our Lord Jesus Christ. Thank You, Holy Father, for allowing Your Son to plead our cases before You on the Day of Judgment. In Your Son's name we come before You, Amen.

—David W. Musick
Lexington, Kentucky

Date Used: _____

The Family Around the Table

Scripture Reading: Galatians 3:26-29

What comes to mind when you think of family? Maybe your thinking turns to Dad, Mom, brother, sister, grandparents, aunt and uncle, vacations, a meal around the table, holiday get-togethers. For some it brings warm thoughts and others much sadness of heart. Yet we all have a concept of family.

It is encouraging to know that no matter what our view of the family may be, we have been adopted as Christians into an eternal family that far exceeds our earthly family.

Paul writes these words to the Galatian family (**read Scripture**).

When assembled around a table, a family demonstrates the picture of family oneness. When we assemble together around the Lord's table, we demonstrate our oneness in Christ, to one another, and the world.

So, when the dinner bell is rung, may we be found around the table with our Father and elder brother who paid the price of adoption for you and me.

Prayer

Father, as we gather around Your table, we remember what family of which we are a part. Thank You, Father, for adopting us into Your eternal family. The price for that adoption is more than we could ever repay. We can only be thankful for that grace which made our adoption possible. In Your Son's name we pray, Amen.

—Ron Camblin
Safety Harbor, Florida

Date Used: _____

The Resurrection:
Today and
Tomorrow

Scripture Reading: 1 Corinthians 11:26

(Read Scripture.)
Paul says that when we come to the Lord's table we proclaim the Lord's death until He comes. In that statement there are two allusions to the resurrection. Neither we nor Paul can think of the death of our Lord without also thinking of His resurrection. Nor can we imagine the return of our Lord without mention of the great resurrection that will occur on that day. There is a great encouragement in the Lord's Supper because it does remind us of the resurrection.

It is true that someday we will arise. But it is not just for the future resurrection that we hope, for the resurrection has already begun. Paul said that by a man came death, and by a man will come the resurrection of the dead (1 Corinthians 15:21). Jesus is the "first fruits" of that resurrection. Though it has not been completed it has already started. From this we gain encouragement in that there is no doubt. The resurrection is a surety.

Yet there is even more encouragement from the Lord's Supper as we see in it the resurrection. In another place Paul writes that if Christ is in us, our bodies are dead because of sin but our spirits are alive because of righteousness (Romans 8:10). Not only has the resurrection begun in us. The same Spirit that raised Christ is even now in us. Though we were dead we are now alive. Even though we are still in mortal bodies, we now have eternal life through His spirit which dwells in us. This is the resurrection as we experience it today.

Prayer

Our Father, as we partake of this Supper, let the resurrection be an encouragement for us to really live. Let our lives show we have experienced a resurrection to new life in Christ Jesus. Lord, please help us continually crucify the old man of sin that is in us. Help us to accept Your promise of a resurrection for both today and tomorrow. In His name, Amen.

—Roy Crowe
Oconee, Georgia

Date Used: _____

Proper Attitude

Scripture Reading: Luke 22:24-27

(Read Scripture.)

Jesus and His disciples celebrated an important Jewish feast, the Passover. During the Passover supper Jesus revealed himself as the ultimate and final sacrificial lamb. His disciples, though unaware of the full significance of what transpired, recognized the serious and solemn attitude of their Master.

Yet, moments after the institution of the Lord's Supper His disciples were found arguing who among them would be the greatest. Besides demonstrating the humanness of the disciples, Luke causes us to reflect upon our own attitudes. When we rise from the Lord's table do we possess an attitude of humility and a willingness to serve? Or are we concerned with the things of the world? The attitude we approach the Lord's Supper with will determine the attitude we leave with. The disciples were unaware of the full significance of what Jesus was doing, but we have the benefit of knowing that Jesus was instituting a memorial feast in honor of His supreme sacrifice.

In his book, *The Cost of Discipleship*, Dietrich Bonheoffer, theologian and martyr, states, "Justification secured our entrance into fellowship and communion with Christ through the unique and final event of his death, and sanctification keeps us in that fellowship in Christ." Here around the Lord's table, we remember that death. And here, the sanctification process is stimulated to continue throughout the week. So let us partake with the sacrifice of our Lord in our thoughts, then arise better able to serve Him whom we honor.

Prayer

Our Lord, this is a solemn moment in our week. Just now we take time to remember the importance of Jesus Christ as the final sacrificial lamb. Help us to have the proper attitude at this time. Let us incorporate humility into our spirits as we commune together. In Your Son's blessed name, Amen.

—Larry E. Green
Grayson, Kentucky

Date Used: _____

Crosses

Scripture Reading: Philippians 2:8

(Read Scripture.)

Think for a moment about our practice of wearing crosses.

Though attractive as jewelry, a gold or silver cross does not project an accurate image of its Christian symbol. Crosses fashioned by craftsmen can be stunning to behold.

The cross of Calvary was anything but beautiful, however. In twenty centuries since the crucifixion, this symbol of suffering and sacrifice has been recast into an object of adornment.

Imagine, if technology had permitted Pilate to use electrocution; and he had sentenced Jesus to die in the electric chair. Would we wear tiny electric chairs on our wrists, around our necks, and on our ears? Would we hang thirty-foot replicas of these high voltage killers above our altars?

We would not. We wouldn't because we know the horror associated with this instrument of death. We have, however, glamorized the rough-hewn wood on which the Savior died.

The cross of Calvary we are to remember is not one of polished gold created by a jewelry designer. Rather, it is the creation of the designer of the universe.

Its value is made precious not by the hands of humans but by the blood of Christ.

As we commune, let us focus on the sacrifice made for us through the body and blood of Christ.

Prayer

Heavenly Father, we see beauty in the cross. The beauty is not in the cumbersome pieces of wood carried by Jesus to Calvary, but in what happened on those pieces of wood. Jesus died a most horrible death—death on a cross—to make us worthy. Help us to fully comprehend both the horror and beauty of this act. In Your Son's name we pray, Amen.

—Rod Irvin
Kingsport, Tennessee

Date Used: _____

Come Unto Me

Scripture Reading: Matthew 4:19

(Read Scripture.)

We usually think of "coming to Jesus" as a one-time experience—at the time of our conversion. Truly, at that time we do "come unto Him."

However, in a larger sense, we must come to Him many, many times later in our life. As we allow the cares of the world and problems of life to separate us from Him, we must come back again and again. He never wavers. He is ever the same. We are the ones who drift away from that first closeness.

Just as we return frequently to our source of supply for nourishing food and refreshing drink of pure water, so we must ever return to the source of supply for our spiritual needs.

We come to Him in spirit and in truth when we bow our heads and hearts in prayer, seeking His will for our lives. We come to Him through worship when we meet together with others of like faith.

We come to Him through knowledge when we study His word. We come to Him through labor when we follow some avenue of Christian service for others.

Probably the closest relationship of all is experienced when we come to Him in the unity of Communion. Christ himself instituted this solemn rite and and said, "This do."

Here at His table, we lay aside for a time anything that would distract or interfere. We can truly "come to Him" here for blessing and fellowship.

Prayer

Our Father, we thank You for this simple act that You have given us. Through this act we can come anew to a closer relationship in fresh commitment, dedicated remembrance, and earnest thanksgiving for Your presence. In His name, we thank You for this memorial feast and for Your continued mercy and grace. Amen.

—Elsie E. Howard
Columbus, Kansas

Date Used: _____

No Sacrifice?

Scripture Reading: Psalm 40:6-8

Psalm 40:6-8 contains a startling claim (**read Scripture**). This assertion is astonishing when we remember that it was made in the Old Testament which was replete with ordinances that required sacrifices and regulated their proper performance. Despite this, our poet was adamant. Sacrifice was neither God's desire nor His demand.

What the Lord really wanted was revealed when the words of this psalm were put into the mouth of Jesus (Hebrews 10:5-7).

As prophecy, this psalm clarifies a fundamental difference between the sacrificial system of the Old Testament and the single sacrifice of the New Testament. Christ's offering at Calvary was not at all like those made under the ancient order. Jesus was now a helpless victim. He was an obedient Son. His sacrifice was different in kind, not just degree. Its effectiveness lay in his obedience, unto death, even the horrible death of the cross (Philippians 2:8). Christ did away with the first order and established the second order (Hebrews 10:9,10).

The emphatic way in which the Hebrew author contrasted the two systems is suggestive. One involved sacrifice (for obedience); the other involved obedience. The first was set aside; the second was established. It was not just Jesus' own obedience that was established, but also that of all who would believe in Him and become children of God (Hebrews 10:16).

Prayer

Lord, at this supper in memory of Jesus' death it is necessary that we repent as well as remember. We repent of our misunderstandings and misbehavior which deny the purpose and betray the power of the cross. To truly discern Christ's death it is essential that we rededicate ourselves to the ultimate purpose for which He died: to redeem us from sin. In Your Son's name we pray, Amen.

—Daer Platt
Houston, Texas

Date Used: _____

Are You Hungry?

Scripture Reading: John 6:35-40

When God made human beings, He
made them with certain hungers. From
early time God has been concerned with
man's hunger. In the wilderness when the
people were hungry, the Lord said to Moses
that He would rain down bread from heav-
en for them (Exodus 16:4). So for a long
time the people ate manna from Heaven.
Jesus was concerned with man's hunger,
as is shown by His feeding the crowds who
were far from home and food. When God
and Jesus saw man's hunger, they met a
present need. However, Jesus showed His
followers that He was more concerned with
spiritual hunger than physical hunger. And
when people are hungry, they should be
fed.

Are you hungry when you come to the
Lord's table? You should be! You should
have a spiritual hunger. After Jesus fed the
crowd of five thousand, the people wanted
to make Him king by force (John 6:5-15).

They were interested only in physical food to satisfy their physical hunger. After Jesus talked about food He declared that He was the bread of life and that anyone who came to him would never go hungry (**read Scripture**).

Jesus desires that no person ever goes hungry—physically or spiritually. But His greater interest is the spiritual, and it should also be ours. So, come to the Lord's table hungry! Go away satisfied, because you have drawn near to Jesus, who feeds the hungry.

Prayer

Our heavenly Father, give us the desire to hunger for spiritual food. Just now we come to Your table to commune in remembrance of Your Son. He is the bread of life. Let us go away from Your table satisfied. Amen.

—J. Fred Bayless
Albuquerque, New Mexico

Date Used: _____

Serving Jesus Only

Scripture Reading: Matthew 17:1-8

Every Lord's Day can be a mountaintop experience for Christians gathered to break the loaf and drink the cup in remembrance of Jesus. Peter, James, and John learned on the mount of transfiguration that Jesus was to have the preeminence over Moses, the lawgiver, and Elijah, the prophet. Peter's rash suggestion that three tabernacles be built to honor the transfigured Jesus and Moses and Elijah, who appeared with Jesus on the mount, was answered by God's solemn voice (**read Scripture**). They fell on their faces with fright, but Jesus consoled them. When they looked up, they saw Jesus only.

In these memorial observances we too need to see Jesus only—not the beauty of the church building nor the seeming ugliness in the lives of those on other pews. There is spiritual refreshment in meditation on Jesus' presence as God's Son. He is our ever-living Savior who came to earth to minister and to give His life as a ransom for our souls.

Because He was willing to pay the price, we can enjoy the forgiveness of our sins and can live a more abundant life, looking forward to His second coming. Indeed, as we pause to see Jesus in our meditations, we do show forth His death until He comes again.

Prayer

Thank You, Father, for seeing our needs and providing through Jesus the opportunity to be Your children. Look into our hearts and forgive us when we fail to put Jesus first in our lives. Bless the loaf and the cup and enable us to see beyond the cares and distractions of this life to the love Jesus demonstrated. Strengthen our conviction that He is the way, the truth, and the life, our strength, and our companion. May we grow and prosper through this spiritual food. In Jesus' name, Amen.

—Earl W. Sims
Cincinnati, Ohio

Date Used: _____

The Effectiveness
of Grace

Scripture Reading: Ephesians 1:7

The radical contrast between the old and new covenants is highlighted by the marked difference in the effect of sin-offerings upon their subjects. Under the law, those sacrifices which they offered over and over did not cleanse the conscience. They only served as reminders of the fact that the worshipers were sinners. Under grace, it is completely different. As we come to the Lord's table, we come to commemorate the wholly-efficacious sacrifice of Christ, which purged our sins to make peace between us and God.

Thus, in the Communion we celebrate our redemption through Christ's blood, rather than, as under Moses, being reminded that we are sinners (**read Scripture**). The Lord's table should be a time for the renewal of one's confidence Godward, as he cleaves to the Savior. Christ disposed of sin

45

by sacrificing himself, obtaining eternal life for us (Hebrews 9:12, 26). We, accordingly, have no more conscience of sins, and are able to worship and serve God without fear.

The confidence which our Lord's reconciliation of us to God is well founded in the complete effectiveness of His sacrifice. That sufficiency, and the confidence which it produces, is exhibited by the triumphant Savior himself. Having made the sacrifice, He sat down on the right hand of God and made His enemies His footstool. Through the one sacrifice of Christ, we are made perfect (Hebrews 1:11-14).

Prayer

Our Father, at the table, we spiritually partake of the body and blood of the Lord. Let us also partake of His confidence in the efficacy of His atonement for sin. Let us be like Abraham and glorify You by our faith and be encouraged and emboldened to serve Him acceptably. Amen.

—Fred O. Blakely
Highland, Indiana

Date Used: _____

Be Imitators of God!

Scripture Reading: Ephesians 5:1, 2

(Read Scripture.)

Be imitators of God! *A carbon copy, to have or assume the appearance of, to follow or try to follow, to produce something which exactly resembles or corresponds to something else, a likeness of the original—* all these are definitions of an imitator.

How many of you know someone to whom you are so close that you can talk like him, write like him, and think like him? To be able to do that means you have to have spent quality time with him. Many hours of sharing are required. When you thoroughly know another person, you can predict what he or she will think about a given situation. You can determine how this person will respond because you know his thinking pattern and his habits.

Paul says we are to be "imitators of Christ." To be an imitator of Christ, we must become like Him. To become like Him means we have to spend quality time with

Him, walking and talking with Him. We have to truly comprehend the price He paid for our redemption. When we can begin to realize the depth of His love for us, then we can truly begin to know Him and strive to be like Him. Each time we meet around His table, let us remember first of all the gift of salvation which He so freely gave to us with no strings attached. Let us also determine to become like Him, His carbon copy.

Prayer

Our gracious heavenly Father, help us to be carbon copies of Christ. Let us mirror His quality of workmanship, His goals, and His ambitions. We know we must strive to be just like our Savior. Let there be a likeness of Christ in our lives. Amen.

—Diane K. Fuller
Bradenton, Florida

Date Used: _____

Clean Heart, Right Spirit, and True Joy

Scripture Reading: Psalm 51:10-12

When Nathan the prophet came before King David, after David had gone unto Bathsheba, the conscience of the king became sorely distressed. David admitted to himself that he had made some very serious breaches in his relationship with God. David had sought delight and pleasure in the humanistic approach to life rather than obeying the Spirit of the Lord. King David became very depressed and sorrowful over his sins. He acknowledged his transgressions, and realized he had sinned against his heavenly Father as well. Then he wrote Psalm 51, verses 10 through 12 (**read Scripture**).

Let us pause for a moment and reflect on our activities during the past week. Could we have sinned and come short of the glory of God? Do we, like David, desire a clean heart, a right spirit, and the joy of God's salvation? These should be our daily objectives, the ultimate desire of every believer.

How can we do this? We have made a

start when we come together in one accord with other believers, on the Lord's Day. When we sing praises of His love, when we pray, and when we hear the sermon, we grow. Through His holy Word, the Holy Spirit convicts us of our sins. As we repent, we can start anew to practice true obedience to the will of our Father. First Corinthians reminds us to proclaim the Lord's death until He returns. We do this every time we take the loaf and drink of the cup. Through these truths, the Lord gives us a clean heart, a right spirit, and the true joy of His salvation.

Prayer

Lord, as we reflect upon our activities of the past week, we must ask ourselves if we have transgressed against Your will. When we come short of Your glory, Lord, show us a clean heart. Show us so that we may desire it. Show us a right spirit that we may be convicted of our sins. Allow us, gracious Father, to experience the joy of Your salvation. In Your Son's name we pray, Amen.

—Bob McPhetridge
Lindsay, California

Date Used: _____

Genuine Love

Scripture Reading: 1 Corinthians 13:4-7

(Read Scripture.)
Love is humanity's most revered ideal. Poets sing its praises. Philosophers and psychologists analyze it. Artists try to portray it. Moralists advocate it as the cure for the world's ills. And everyone in his or her own way strives to get, or to give, love.

But what is love—genuine love?

Perhaps we can explain love by telling what love does. First Corinthians 13, a familiar Scripture passage, depicts love in terms of how the loving person relates to others in humility, patience, and service. Love gives, and gives freely, making sacrifices for the ones loved.

The Bible describes love, but it goes beyond mere definition. The Bible reveals love by describing love's supreme sacrifice. God shows what love is, by what He has done. God gave His only Son so that we could live forever (John 3:16).

In the Lord's Supper we see emblems of

God's amazing love. For, here we see reminders of Jesus' death. The loaf reminds us of the body of Christ, broken for our salvation. The red contents of the cup speak to us of the shed blood of the crucified Savior.

Here we witness the depth of God's love for us. We can measure the extent of His love by the price He paid for our salvation. That price was the suffering and death of His Son.

Prayer

Lord, here at the Lord's table, let us behold God's love. Let us find our love ignited by His example. Let us love him, as we perceive how great is His love for us. Let us pledge Him our lives in service in return. In Your Son's name we pray, Amen.

—Tom Lane
Cincinnati, Ohio

Date Used: _____

Mercy, Not Sacrifice

Scripture Reading: Matthew 12:1-8

(Read Scripture.)

In Matthew 12:2 we learn that some Pharisees complained to Jesus that His disciples were breaking the Sabbath by picking some heads of grain and eating them. Jesus responded, "I desire mercy, not sacrifice." In saying this, Jesus quoted Hosea 6:6. What Jesus said is that sacrifice is not an end, but a means to an end—mercy.

Mercy is translated from the Hebrew word *hesed*. It was most frequently used to describe God in the Old Testament. It was therefore the chief word describing godliness. *Hesed* incorporated two major thoughts: first, it was the very performing of covenant terms; secondly, it was promoting the best interests of the other, according to the covenant. In other words, it's promoting God's best interests as well as your neighbor's.

The Jews were very self-righteous in their own eyes for keeping even the smallest detail of the law. But by the time Jesus arrived on the scene, they had almost totally lost sight of looking after the best interests of others, including God.

What might this have to do with the Lord's Supper today? Is it possible that Jesus would say to us, "I desire mercy—*hesed*—not the Lord's Supper?" The Lord's Supper is an ordinance of God calculated to assist us in becoming faithful Christians. It serves as a means to an end, not an end in itself. Mechanically going through the motions of observing the Lord's Supper when unaccompanied by Christlike living, or *hesed*, is as unacceptable to God as were the sacrifices of the Jews when unaccompanied by godliness.

Prayer

Our Father, as we commune today, help us focus our thoughts on Your Son's life. We ask You to help us become more like Yourself. As we become more like You, help us to begin to exhibit mercy or *hesed*, something You have wanted of Your people all throughout history. Amen.

—Jeffery G. Trabold
O'Fallon, Missouri

Date Used: _____

The Invitation
Is His!

Scripture Reading: 1 Corinthians 11:24-26

(Read Scripture.)
Our Communion service is often called the Lord's Supper. It is His Supper, prepared by Him for sinners like you and me. Christians are forgiven and that is what the Lord's Supper brings to mind.

We are not worthy, but He invites us to partake of the loaf, which represents His body broken for us, and the cup, which represents His blood shed for us. Because of His broken body and shed blood, we, though sinners, may have the forgiveness of our sins and share eternal life with Him.

The supper invitation is His! No one else has the right to invite and no one can exclude anyone from partaking.

If your best friend prepared a meal at great price and invited you, would you refuse to attend? Jesus Christ, your best friend, has, at great cost, prepared this meal for us to share with Him. It cost Him His life, and He desires and expects us to attend.

Regrets and excuses are not acceptable. The place He has prepared for you cannot be filled by anyone else. He has promised to meet with us and bless us.

A beautiful hymn by Mary Ann Lathbury says:

> *Break Thou the bread of life,*
> *Dear Lord to me,*
> *As Thou didst break the loaves*
> *beside the sea;*
> *Beyond the sacred page*
> *I seek Thee, Lord;*
> *My spirit pants for Thee,*
> *O living Word."*

Prayer

Dear Father, we know that the Lord's Supper is not a one-time event. For as the physical body needs continued nourishment, so the spiritual body needs continued spiritual food, in order to remain alive and well. Thank You, Father, for the spiritual food You provide for us.

—Lillian P. King
Maysville, Kentucky

Date Used: _____

56

Disturbing Communion

Scripture Reading: Mark 14:17-21

Our meeting at the Lord's table is an occasion for quiet reflection and a thankful memory. It is also an occasion of warning and deep disturbance.

It was surely disturbing enough when Jesus met with the twelve in the upper room. That was the night in which Jesus was betrayed (see 1 Corinthians 11:23). Mark tells of it in his chapter 14, verses 17-21 (**read Scripture**). It was not a matter to be taken lightly, then or now, that the Lord should be betrayed by one of His own, who had eaten with Him at the table. Yet before that night was over, two—not one—of the twelve would defect. One—Simon Peter—would say, "I don't know Him." The other—Judas Iscariot—would say in effect, "I know Him all right. I know Him well enough to find Him in the dark. But just now I'd rather have money than Jesus. So give me money and you can take Jesus."

Does Jesus need again this morning to

warn and disturb us by saying that before this day—or at least this week—is over some who meet with Him now at His table will deny by word or deed that they know Him? Does He need to warn again that others will say by word or deed, "Oh, I know Jesus well enough. For years I have been a member of a church with His name on it. But for now I'd really rather have something else. So give me that something else I'd rather have, and at least for now you can take Jesus and do with Him whatever you please"?

It is not an occasion for complacency. It is enough to cause any of us to gasp, "Master, is it I?"

Prayer

Heavenly Father, You are our Redeemer. Let us reflect; let us remember. Let us walk away mindful of the warning that Jesus gave to His disciples: "One of you will betray me." We are disturbed by this warning. However, Lord, though we have all betrayed You in our lifetimes, You still provide this memorial to show us Your grace. In Your Son's name we pray, Amen.

—Edwin V. Hayden
Cincinnati, Ohio

Date Used: _____

He Became Sin

Scripture Reading: 2 Corinthians 5:21

We are often reminded at Communion time of the unique ability of Jesus to understand His people. Jesus can understand us because He was just like us, tempted in all ways that we are, but without sin. But one thing I've thought that Jesus couldn't possibly understand is guilt. How could one without sin understand the guilt and remorse that come with sin? Even after asking God for forgiveness, many of us are plagued with guilt and a feeling of unworthiness before the Lord. Often our feelings become obsessive to the point of sin in themselves.

A Scripture comes to mind. In 2 Corinthians 5:21 we read (**read Scripture**).

I realized that as Jesus hung on that cross, He became sin. He didn't bear just my sins. He didn't even take just the sins of the most grievous murderer. Instead, he took the sin of all time to the cross along with the guilt and remorse brought by all that evil. He knew to the depth of His being what kind of separation and pain come with sin. God turned away from His only begotten Son and showed us plainly what sin accomplishes.

Because of Jesus, we become the righteousness of God. We are no longer unworthy before Him. When He looks at us, He sees Jesus.

Communion is a time of celebration. We remember the guilt of our sin, realizing that Jesus took the whole ugly mess to the cross. Now we rejoice that we are the righteousness of God in Him.

Prayer

Lord, our blessed Redeemer, You came to earth to show us who You are. You are perfect in all ways. We are imperfect. Despite our guilt You became sin—the sin for which we should have died. Now Jesus can be seen in us. Amen.

—Claudia J. Lee
Philomath, Oregon

Date Used: _____

The Image of Jesus

Scripture Reading: Romans 8:29

A French sculptor was carving a bust of Ralph Waldo Emerson. During the fourth sitting, Emerson came over and stood next to the artist. He gazed long and thoughtfully at the unfinished work. Finally, he said with a smile, "The trouble is that the more it resembles me, the worse it looks."

The Christian stands back and looks at his own life. After thoughtful examination, he admits, "The more my life resembles me, the worse it looks." But the more it resembles Jesus, the better it is. Paul once said that Christians are to conform to the image of Jesus Christ (**read Scripture**).

The image of Jesus is not a statue or a portrait—even though Pope Gregory claimed about A. D. 730 that Christ himself had sent His own picture to a local king! The image of Jesus is not a physical likeness, but a moral likeness. To be conformed to the image of Jesus, we must begin living by the principles He taught.

The Lord's Supper provides an event whereby Christians reflect on being conformed to Jesus' image. This is both personal and corporate because many brethren are involved. We help each other. We uplift one another. Coming to this table is a testimony that we desire the company of God's people and conformity to God's Son.

Prayer

Wonderful Father, we know we have been created in Your image. The more we resemble You, the more worthy we are of Your grace. Assist us, Father, as we daily struggle to conform to the image of Your Son, Jesus Christ. Remind us to encourage each other in an effort to be more like You. In Your Son's name we pray, Amen.

—John M. Boberg
Crystal Lake, Illinois

Date Used: _____

The Unique Sacrifice of Jesus

Scripture Reading: Romans 5:7

(Read Scripture.)

While we talk and read and pray about the sacrifice Jesus made, seldom do we stop to consider just what that sacrifice included. At first glance it would not seem any greater than many individuals have made since that time. Many martyrs have willingly given up their lives in espousal of a good cause. All these are commendable sacrifices. However, on deeper reflection, we see a marked difference in the sacrifice of Jesus.

Many heroic sacrifices are spontaneous, without time to consider the consequences. Jesus spent all His years of accountability knowing that He must die for the sins of others. He willingly involved himself in an ever-deepening controversy that would surely lead to death. He spent strenuous days and sleepless nights ministering to the very individuals who would deny Him.

Lesser mortals will make the supreme sacrifice in military service or in the realization that a loved one or a cherished ideal is in peril, yet Jesus willingly gave His life that even the vilest and least deserving might be redeemed. Humans may display unnatural valor or bravery because of a sense of guilt or feeling of insufficiency in their past lives, but Jesus was sinless. He acted only because of His love for all mankind and His desire to do His Father's will.

As we hold the loaf and cup in our memorial to our Lord, let us remember that His sacrifice was truly unique in the history of God's creation. It surely merits our fullest measure of love and service.

Prayer

Our heavenly Father, many times we say that we would lay down our lives for others. However, that boast is full of conditions. We would hesitate to die for perhaps a stranger, a villain, or an enemy. Jesus' death was unconditional. He knew that the purpose of His life surrounded His death and willingly went to the cross for all people. Lord, just now we thank You for the unique sacrifice of Jesus Christ. We have perhaps denied Jesus many times in our lives, but we are thankful that He did not deny us.

—Howard Utterback
West Union, Illinois

Date Used: _____

In Our Defense

Scripture Reading: 1 John 2:1, 2

You may not be so thrilled at the number of guilty offenders who seem to get off because of some loophole in our puzzling legal system. Scripturally, we find a very different kind of lawyer who speaks on our behalf in the very courts of Heaven (**read Scripture**).

We see here that Jesus appears before the Father in our defense whenever we win. Unlike Perry Mason, He is not looking for the real culprit for we are guilty. There is no hope of a slick lawyer's finding a legal loophole, for none exist before Almighty God. Jesus speaks in our defense despite our guilt. And the only reason He does so is because He himself has already paid the penalty for our sins.

As we gather to partake of the Lord's Supper, let us remember the great price paid that our sins may be forgiven. Let us remember Him who died and faithfully intercedes for us, even now when we stumble. Let us remember that His atoning sacrifice is intended for the sins of all. Let us use this time to renew our commitment to Him and to the task He has given us—to win the lost to Him.

Prayer

Merciful Father, we thank You for our defender, Jesus Christ. What would we do without Him? Because You have provided for our defense, we gain that hope for eternal life with You, Lord. Amen.

—Dan Nicksich
Barryton, Michigan

Date Used: _____

Discipleship
for Jesus

Scripture Reading: 1 Corinthians 3:21-23

Many gatherings around this table are less than they could be. Tremendous joy and encouragement are absent because we fail to recognize and accept the grace of God given to the whole church.

Paul, the apostle, once wrote to a group of Christians who had divided over different loyalties. Some aspect of the grace of Jesus had caught their fancy and their devotion to that one aspect had caused them to discount or even deny other aspects of His grace.

Paul had to remind them that in their limited devotion they had lost the fullness of Jesus. Paul wrote (**read Scripture**).

It is good to remember as we gather here that our discipleship is toward Jesus. It is of Him that we eat and drink. He is our sustenance. Therefore all He gives we accept.

As we prepare to partake, let's determine to accept the gift of God in all its packaging so that we will really rejoice when He comes to claim all that are His.

Jesus gave a new command to His disciples. He said that they must love each other as He loved them. If they did this, everyone would recognize them as His disciples (John 13:34, 35). Can others see the love in you and recognize you as a follower of Christ?

Prayer

Holy God, we come before You as sinful people. Let us not boast in men, but help us to realize that our discipleship is toward Jesus and Jesus only. We accept what He gives. Let others recognize that our discipleship is toward Jesus by the love we have for one another. Amen.

—Charles Mosley
Sulsun, California

Date Used: _____

Continual
Commitment

Scripture Reading: Matthew 4:18-22;
26:40, 41

(Read Scripture.)
Commitment is a lifetime proposition. By
comparing these two passages we can see
how hard it was for even Jesus' disciples to
maintain their level of commitment. After
all, hadn't they left everything to follow
Christ? How much more committed could
they be? How we envy their position.
Haven't we all thought to ourselves how
much easier it would be to live the Christian life if we had been able to walk and
talk with the Master as His disciples did?
Yet we see here that it wasn't all that easy
for them either. Just when Jesus needed
them most, they failed Him.

The temptation is there for us to justify
our own lack of commitment by comparing
ourselves to the disciples rather than
Christ. They had times of failure. How can

we be any better? But the story continues. After Pentecost, the disciples received power from the Holy Spirit to finally experience the level of commitment they had witnessed in Jesus. This is the same Holy Spirit we have available to us today.

Jesus took our place on the cross so we could take His place in the world. As we think about Jesus and His total commitment to the cause of saving the world, let's examine our own level of commitment. Are we watching and praying, or are we asleep in the garden?

Prayer

Precious Father, it is so easy to make excuses for our own failures. Because Jesus does not bodily walk today as He did two thousand years ago, we justify our lack of commitment by saying, "If only Jesus were on the earth today; His disciples were so lucky to see Him in person." We have the Holy Spirit just as His disciples did. Lord, we ask that you continually rest your spirit on us as it nurtures our commitment to you. In Your Son's name, Amen.

—Philip James Gould
Liscomb, Iowa

Date Used: _____

70

Growth in Grace

Scripture Reading: Galatians 3:11-15

Jewish legalism insisted that you had to earn God's approval by circumcision and keeping all sorts of ceremonial laws. Paul gave another message to the Galatian church (**read Scripture**). He never tired of preaching the liberating message, the "good news." He had a difficult time understanding why so many Galatians had fallen back into the old ways of doing things and were depending on the works of the law to earn their salvation.

We must understand that we are being redeemed. God began a good work in our lives when we were born of water and the Spirit (John 3:1-7). We were forgiven of every sin (Romans 8:1). He who began this good work has power to see it through to completion. That is our hope! However, at this moment we are not completed projects. We are souls under construction. Many battles have been fought and won, but the war is not over (Romans 7:15-25).

An ancient monk in explaining activity in the monastery said, "We fall down and we get up. We fall down and we get up. We fall down and we get up." We grow when we get up. Or put another way, we grow when we resolve again to be more of what we want to be and less of what we used to be (Philippians 3:12-16).

We have not arrived, but God is full of mercy and patience and He has not given up on us yet! We press on. We mature—slowly and gradually and through falling and rising again, we look forward to the best (Revelation 2:10).

As we remember our Lord, by breaking the bread and partaking of the fruit of the vine, we grow in grace and knowledge.

Prayer

Heavenly Father, we thank You for Your grace. Many times we fall short of true Christian maturity, but Your grace allows us to pick up the pieces and grow in You. Help us to daily grow in grace and knowledge. Amen.

—L. Palmer Young
Lexington, Kentucky

Date Used: _____

Trudging
Weary Paths

Scripture Reading: Luke 24:25

(Read Scripture.)

The two trudged the weary path toward a place called home. Downcast, they told their tale to a traveler who fell in step. A friend had been executed. He was a good man and had been stricken down in his prime. His destroyed potential, a loss tragic to many friends, left behind a crushing grief. They trudged onward toward the night.

Their heavy hearts wept for hope aborted. Their burdened spirits longed for encouragement. Their sagging faith explored the bottom. The traveler spoke, but their preoccupation kept him distant. They really wanted to accept his words of consolation. They did at least invite him to their table. They asked him to bless the bread. His grace, fitting and good, touched their hearts. Their downcast eyes looked upward. They then beheld Him for the first time.

In His grace, the dikes protecting their fragile spirits crumbled. In flooded a healing torrent. They rushed out and returned urgently to the path. This time, however, they stepped lightly. Even in the darkness, they felt the advent of day. Their soaring spirits hastened them on the journey. Faith lifted them to live in scorn of consequences. They sought community. They needed a place to confess wholeheartedly that the Lord has risen!.

For almost two thousand years now we have trudged weary paths toward places we call home. Today we often find ourselves with heavy hearts, crushed spirits and a weary faith. Preoccupations still keep Him distant. With the dust from the Emmaus path still on their exhausted feet, these seekers welcomed His blessing at their table. In His good grace, He resurrected their lives. Their trudge then became a march of proclamation. Let us ever recall that, even though He had journeyed with them on the way, they first beheld Him in the breaking of the bread.

Prayer

Our Father, sin has crushed our spirits, but You have lifted the guilt from us. Open our eyes so that we can see the hope that lies ahead—eternal life with You.

—Donald A. Twist
Indianapolis, Indiana

Date Used: _____

The Good Shepherd

Scripture Reading: John 10:11

What is meant by going through the "valley of the shadow of death"? Is it dying? It may be. It may be living day by day with threats not only to our present life here but to our eternal life if we let the forces of evil lead us astray. But whichever it is, we need fear no evil because God is with us. He is the shepherd. Jesus said (**read Scripture**).

It is because He is the Good Shepherd, because He did lay down His life for His sheep that we are here now about to partake of these emblems that represent His body and His blood. The emblems are evidence that He gave His life because He loves His sheep. One difference between that shepherd and any other is that if any of us were to give his life for the sheep, the sheep might be in worse condition than before because there would be no shepherd! But the Good Shepherd not only gave His life for us, but rose from the dead and He is our shepherd today. He beckons us to walk with Him until we can be with Him in eternity. Let us remember as we "walk through the valley of the shadow of death," we need fear no evil because the Good Shepherd is with us."

As we partake of these emblems, let's remember how God has loved us, how the Shepherd gave His life for His sheep.

Prayer

Lord God, we rejoice that You loved us so greatly that You became the Good Shepherd, knowing that the Good Shepherd would suffer and die to save the sheep. We rejoice again that You conquered death by dying. Thank You for shepherding us still through the valley of the shadow of death. May this remembrance of what You have done and what You are doing dispel our fear of evil and motivate our living to bring honor to Your name. Amen.

—Vaughn Ross
Columbus, Ohio

Date Used: _____

His Name Is Jesus

Scripture Reading: Matthew 1:21

What's in a name? We give our children names for identification purposes, but in Bible days a name had a very special meaning for the person. For example: Abram became Abraham; Sarai became Sarah; Jacob became Israel. Even the name of God was written in consonants and spoken in low breath that His name would not be blasphemed. The consonants were JHVH. Later the vowels were added to form the word Jehovah. The prophets and the psalmists added many names for the coming Messiah, all of which befitted His personality and authority on earth.

An angel of the Lord appeared to Joseph in a dream and said (**read Scripture**). The name of Jesus shall be above all other names. It is the one whereby we might be saved (Acts 4:12). "Jesus" might be the name we carry in our hearts daily. We remember Him by gathering at His "love feast," as often as we meet to partake of the emblems of His suffering on Calvary's cross.

Jesus asks that we partake of the cup which He says is His blood shed for the remission of our sins and the loaf which is His body broken for us. Let us humbly remember His name in our witness for Him.

Prayer

Father, we give You thanks, honor, and glory for the sacrificial gift of Jesus Christ for the pardoning of our sins, and the assurance of His resurrection that He is with us always. In His holy name, Amen.

—Bill Humphrey
Cincinnati, Ohio

Date Used: _____

The Best Way
to Remember

Scripture Reading: Hebrews 6:4-6

(Read Scripture.)

We are called together each Lord's Day to remember. The most important events so far on this planet took place on Calvary and at the tomb. Lest we stray away God wants us to remember these events each Lord's Day.

The God who made more stars than we can see, more grains of sand than we can count, more ocean than the fish can use, also gave us the best way to remember His love.

We can observe an empty cross and for a short time remember. We can hear a Communion meditation and soon forget. God's love, foresight, and knowledge stretches to make this event memorable:

1. We hear the meditation.
2. We see the emblems.

3. We smell the emblems.
4. We touch the emblems.
5. We taste the emblems.

God stimulates all of our senses to make the great events of the past unforgettable to those who love Him. We cannot outdo God when it comes to planning our form of worship.

Prayer

Our holy God, we come here and remember the events at Calvary. You have provided the best possible way to remember these events. We hear the Word. We see, smell, touch and taste the emblems. Help us to keep all of our senses focused on You. In Your Son's name we pray, Amen.

—Brent Theophilus
Mount Vernon, Ohio

Date Used: _____

The Nature
and Purpose
of Communion

Scripture Reading: Amos 5:21-24

(Read Scripture.)

Nothing injures the church more than allowing the Lord's Supper to become as the religious feasts spoken of in Amos. We can prevent this by letting two thoughts always be present concerning this holy Communion — the nature and purpose of Communion and the duty to commune.

The nature and purpose of Communion is to proclaim the Lord's death until He comes (1 Corinthians 11:26). Proclaiming the Lord's death as the Redeemer of the world, we confess our belief in Him. To confess our belief in Him, we say to the world, "I have chosen to follow Him." Proclaiming that we are His followers, we enter into an obligation to be obedient to all He has taught.

This is the cup of the New Covenant. He that breaks the conditions of a covenant, dissolves his side of the covenant. Which of us have not sinned? Sin separates man from God. God in His wisdom knew we would continually need to reaffirm our side of the covenant. The Lord's Supper is a ratification of the covenant on my part, after having alienated myself from God by sin.

As His child, I have a need for constant devotion. All ideas influence my desires, either good or bad. If I allow a bad desire to conceive, it gives birth to sin. If I allow a good desire to conceive, it gives birth to holiness. However, all ideas lose their force in time unless revived. By dwelling on ideas or thoughts, I may increase their force. Thus, to meditate upon good brings victory over evil and the results are holiness.

As followers of Jesus, how then can we not be obedient to the command to be holy? Who could not respond to the call of duty to commune with their Lord?

Prayer

Father, help us who are weak to understand the importance of a constant remembrance of the death of Your Son. Help us, Father, to see its blessing and its benefits. Amen.

—Gene M. Langley
Chesapeake, Virginia

Date Used: _____

84

We, the Royal Priesthood

Scripture Reading: Matthew 27:50, 51

(Read Scripture.)

As you know, the Communion service is one of the most important parts of our worship. Together we partake of the loaf and cup in remembrance of the body and blood of Christ our Savior. We remember that our sins were laid upon Him and nailed to the cross with Him. We are no longer under condemnation to the guilt, penalty, or bondage of sin. Christ instituted this memorial service to keep these facts focused on our minds.

You would think that something as vital to us as the Communion service is, would have pages of instruction written about it in the Bible. This is not so. Actually, there are only 89 verses in the New Testament having to do with the subject. Of these, only 33 verses directly give instruction and information concerning the Communion service.

Some knowledge of the Lord's table was given to us when God had Moses and the Israelites build the tabernacle following their deliverance from bondage in Egypt.

The tabernacle was divided into two rooms, divided by a veil. Only the high Priest was allowed to enter the second room which was called the Holy of Holies. The first room, the Holy Place, contained a lampstand, altar of incense, and a table of showbread. The priests kept the lamp burning and the smoke of the incense going up continually. On each Sabbath day, they would eat the bread on the table of showbread.

Everything about the tabernacle pictured what was to take place when Christ came to earth to establish His church. We, the royal priesthood of Christ's church, are to keep the light of Christ glowing to enlighten the church and the world. Our prayers are to go up before God in Heaven. On every Lord's Day, we are to eat the bread and drink the cup in remembrance of the body and blood of our Lord.

Prayer

Our God in Heaven, You are the same from age to age. We, Your royal priesthood, just now offer prayers to You, Lord, and we keep the light of Your church glowing for all to see. Help us to remember the body and blood of Christ. Amen.

—Everett McGee
Ashland, Oregon

Date Used: _____

New Life Created

Scripture Reading: Galatians 2:20

During the Communion service we remember, among other things, the death of Jesus on a cross. His life was faultless, but His death was just as complete as any death ever was. Paul declared in Galatians 2:20 (**read Scripture**).

In his book, *The Road Less Traveled*, Dr. Scott Peck attempts to impart some wisdom and insight into the problem of living at peace with ourselves and the world. In a discourse on discipline he states, "In the present day Western culture, the self is held sacred and death is considered an unspeakable insult. Yet the exact opposite is the reality. It is in the giving up of self that human beings can find the most ecstatic and lasting, solid, durable joy of life. And it is death that provides life with all its meaning."

Whether he meant to or not, this psychiatrist paraphrased Paul's new life statement and caught the essence of Jesus' response to Nicodemus. Christ told him that he must be born again (John 3:3).

The old self-centered personality must die. It must be purposefully put to death. A new life can then be created that is Christ-centered, God-centered. Jesus lived this kind of God-centered life when He was here with us. He did not have to die either physically or spiritually but He did. It is this unnecessary, yet necessary, death that we remember by partaking of the bread and fruit of the vine at this moment. Jesus was speaking to all of us when He stated that He had come to give us life and have that life more abundantly (John 10:10).

Prayer

Our most heavenly Father, we have been crucified with Christ and we no longer live, but Christ lives in us. We know, Father, that we should set aside self-centered ambitions and live Christ-centered lives. Help us to give of our lives, just as Jesus Christ gave of His. In Your Son's name, Amen.

—Daryl Stroad
Bristol, Virginia

Date Used: _____

Jesus Washes
Our Feet

Scripture Reading: John 13:4,5

Taking Communion is an amazing privilege. No matter what we are experiencing, be it grace or difficulty, Jesus allows us to stop and remember that He loves us. He loves us so much that He died so that we can be clean before a righteous God.

Communion is a time when Jesus says, "Let me wash your feet." In John 13, Jesus and His disciples were getting ready to eat their last meal together. Then Jesus did something extraordinary (**read Scripture**).

Jesus began washing His disciples' feet on the same night He instituted Communion. Foot washing prepared a person to enter into the house. Likewise, letting Jesus "wash our feet" as we confess our sins before we take Communion, prepares us to enter into God's very presence.

Foot washing was what servants of the lowest rank did. Imagine Jesus honoring

His disciples that way! Jesus never tires of washing our feet because He is the ultimate servant. He died so that we can have fellowship like He does with His Father.

Jesus even washed Judas' feet—Judas, who was scheming to betray Him! There's nothing you have done that He isn't willing to forgive. We must follow His example by loving one another enough to forgive one another. Take some time now while the servers come to pass the bread and juice, to let Jesus wash your feet.

Prayer

Heavenly Father, we are humbled at the thought of our Savior, Jesus Christ, washing our feet. Yet that is what He does when we remember His sacrifice. Thank You for the example He has shown us. Amen.

—Gina Watumull
Honolulu, Hawaii

Date Used: _____

A Costly Offering

Scripture Reading: Hebrews 10:10, 12, 14

David had blown it. He decided to do something that God had forbidden: take a census of Israel. But after it was finished, he knew he had sinned (2 Samuel 24:10).

God's punishment for David's disobedience was a pestilence. For three days it raged. During that time 70,000 men died. Then God stopped at the threshing floor of Araunah. David was told by the prophet Gad to go up to the threshing floor and erect an altar to the Lord. He did and when he saw Araunah he offered to buy the threshing floor.

But Araunah wouldn't accept payment. He offered the threshing floor, the oxen, the sledges, and the yokes for free. David refused. He would only buy them for a price (2 Samuel 24:24)

Isn't that amazing? David knew that an offering had to cost something in order to be effective. And isn't that what God expects out of all of us because that is what

He did himself? This Communion table ought to remind us of that fact every week. Here is the body of Christ which is given for us. A costly offering. Here is the cup that is poured out for us, the new covenant in His blood—a costly offering.

As the writer of Hebrews says (**read Scripture**).

The costly sacrifice was effective. We now have a place in Heaven. This Communion is a time to rejoice as we remember the offering, the costly offering, of Jesus Christ.

Prayer

Most gracious God in Heaven, help us to remember the costly offering You used to save us. We know that nothing we do, say, or offer will make up for that sacrifice. Nevertheless we can offer nothing less than our whole lives as an offering to You. In Your Son's name, Amen.

—J. B. Straus, Jr.
Dallas, Texas

Date Used: _____

Meditations for
Special Days

Starting Anew
(New Year's Day)

Scripture Reading: 1 Corinthians 11:26

The beginning of a new year is traditionally a time of looking back at the old and looking ahead to the new—a time of self-examination. Recognizing the accomplishments and the failures of the past, we determine to do better in the year to come. Unhappily, human frailty being what it is, those resolutions are often broken all too soon.

We don't have to wait for another New Year's Day to start fresh again. The Lord offers the opportunity for such self-examination and resolution much more often than once a year. First Corinthians 11:26, 28 reads (**read Scripture**).

Self-examination, if it is honest, can be very painful. Out of the pain of seeing our sin for what it is and acknowledging it to God comes the cleansing that brings the freedom to live aright.

Not only does the Lord forgive and cleanse, but He also helps in our resolutions to do better. We don't have to try to do it all ourselves. Paul told the Philippians that the Lord was working in them (Philippians 2:12, 13). He is at work in us as well.

With His help we can resolve to live righteously and godly one week—no, one day—at a time. For although the supper of the Lord is a time of reflection and resolve, we can go to Him daily in prayer, confessing our sin, and receiving cleansing and new resolve to live the godly life to which He calls us.

Prayer

Lord, as we begin a New Year help us as we resolve to live righteously and godly every day for the new year. Only with Your help can we do this. Guide us in our times of self-examination and periods of spiritual growth. Amen.

—Rebecca Souder
Derby, Kansas

Date Used: _____

How Time Flies!
(Easter Sunday)

Scripture Reading: Psalm 90:4

(Read Scripture.)

How time flies!

It seemed only yesterday we were throwing out the wrappings and stowing away the gifts of Christmas. Only yesterday we were celebrating the season of Christ's birth, sharing again the glad tidings of great joy that accompanied Immanuel—God with us.

And now, we remember His death.

Time flies.

It must have seemed that way to Mary at the crucifixion. In a matter of a few short hours her son had been betrayed, blasphemed, and battered. Through tear-stained eyes the passing of His thirty-three years must have seemed to her, a blur. Time flies.

It might have seemed that way to Jesus' Father. To God, a thousand years is as a day. Generations have come and gone and God's day is only just begun. The short time He spent among us in the person of Jesus was only the smallest fraction of His eternal timetable, but it represented the glorious dawning of a new and better day. Time flies.

It seems that way to us, too. From Christmas to Easter, from birth to death, life at best is brief. We need the constant reminder that is the Lord's Supper. He who came, is coming again. Time flies.

Prayer

Lord, not very long ago we celebrated the birth of Your Son. Now, at this time of the year, we observe His death and resurrection. Time passes by quickly, Lord, and sometimes we get so involved with our lives. We need a constant reminder of the resurrection, not just around Easter, but every Lord's Day. Amen.

—Stevan Terrance McClure
Sevierville, Tennessee

Date Used: _____

An Indebtedness
Passed
(Mother's Day)

Scripture Reading: 2 Timothy 1:5

Each of us here today is indebted to countless numbers of people for what we have. We are indebted to inventors such as Thomas Edison, Alexander Graham Bell, the Wright brothers, and to Henry Ford.

On a more personal level, however, we are indebted to those who raised us. In 2 Timothy 1:5 the apostle Paul informs us that Timothy was indebted to his mother and grandmother for the example of faith that they instilled in him (**read Scripture**).

Each time we partake of Communion we proclaim to our family, friends, and those around us the significance of Jesus' death and our indebtedness to Him for it.

In the Old Testament the Jews celebrated the Passover annually so that each generation would remember God's deliverance of their forefathers from Egypt (Exodus 13:8).

A wise person once said, "Christianity is only one generation from becoming extinct." Let us thank our mothers for instilling the faith in us. As we eat the feast today, let us meditate upon the debt Christ paid for us and remember the example we are setting as we partake.

God forbid that this remembrance ever stop.

Prayer

Father God, we thank You for Christian mothers—those who have fulfilled their honorable God-given role to bring us up in the way of the Lord. As we partake of the Supper today may it not just be a proclamation of what we have been taught but a faith of our own. Help us to remember that each time we eat and drink of the emblems we are proclaiming to family, friends, and those around us the Lord's death. In Jesus' name, Amen.

—Brian Waldrop
Champaign, Illinois

Date Used: _____

The Price of
Freedom
(Memorial Day)

Scripture Reading: Luke 22:7-16

(Read Scripture.)

It was Memorial Day and the newspaper was lying open on the front porch. It showed the picture of a young widow placing flowers on the grave of her late husband who had given his life in the service of his country. Looking on was their young son. We could only wonder what she had said to their son about his father and the price he had paid for their freedom.

It was the time of the Passover and Jesus had said to Peter and John to go and prepare the Passover so that they could eat (Luke 22:8). Final preparations having been made, Jesus said that he desired to eat the Passover meal with them before He suffered (Luke 22:15).

Following the Passover meal when they

had remembered their deliverance from Egyptian bondage He took the bread and broke it. He said, "This is my body." With the cup, He said, "This is my blood." It was the first day of the week and the disciples were assembled to "break bread" to remind them of their deliverance from sin by the sacrifice of Jesus. This gave Paul an opportunity to preach to them (Acts 20:7). We hold dear the tradition of the Christians of the first century as we continue the practice of observing the Lord's Supper, on the Lord's Day, in the Lord's house.

What a tremendous price He paid for our sins! As we eat the bread and drink the cup we celebrate our salvation. Let us then remember Jesus as He instructed us. He is the lamb of God who came to take away the sins of the world.

Prayer

Father, Jesus paid a price for our freedom. We were slaves to sin, but Jesus gave all so that we could be acceptable to You. Just now we remember this price that was paid, and we thank you that You did not make us pay that price. In Your Son's name, Amen.

—Wilbur A. Reid, Sr.
Johnson City, Tennessee

Date Used: _____

Supper With
the Father
(Father's Day)

Scripture Reading: Matthew 11:27

(Read Scripture.)

It's meal time. Mother tells Daddy, "Supper is about ready. Better get the children in." So Daddy puts down his paper and rounds up the children from their play. "Get your hands washed. Supper is ready. Hurry up." He helps the little ones climb up on the box so they can reach the sink. Then when everyone is in a high chair or pulled up to the table, the family begins the meal.

When we come to Communion, here too the family gathers around the table. The Father has prepared it to honor his eldest Son. He calls, "Supper is ready. Come and be washed. Come to supper." It is the best time of all when we share together and tell the Father of all our activities of the day.

We rejoice in the good things that have happened and confess the mistakes we made. Then He smiles and says, "I'll help you try to do better next time. I love you just the same."

Then there is the sad look that comes over the Father's face when He looks around the table. All the family are not here. "Where are the rest of the children? Have they forgotten?" The call goes out again. "Supper is ready. Come and be washed. Come to supper. Hurry!"

Prayer

Father, we often forget that we truly are Your children. Thank You for loving us even when we fail. We are family and we are comforted to know You will protect us as Your children. Just now we gather at Your Table to remember the offering of Your Son—a testimony of how much You are willing to sacrifice as our Father. Amen.

—Joyce E. Vance
Grand Junction, Colorado

Date Used: _____

Spiritual Freedom
(Independence Day)

Scripture Reading: Romans 6:18

(Read Scripture.)

In 1776, our forefathers signed a "Declaration of Independence" from England. For the next six years the men of the American Colonies fought the Revolutionary War to assure us of that freedom from bondage to the mother country.

Almost 2,000 years ago, mankind gained spiritual independence from life under the law when God gave His beloved Son to suffer and die on the cross on our behalf and free us from the bondage of animal sacrifices. We have only to answer the question, "Shall we put our trust in Christ and accept Him as our Savior or shall we not?" To accept Christ as our Savior means life abundant—life that shall never end. To reject Christ means hopelessness—eternal death.

We will be celebrating Independence Day

this week with parades, picnics, and fireworks. We commemorate our spiritual independence each Sunday by reverently partaking of the broken bread representing the broken body of Jesus and drinking from the cup representing the blood that He shed for us. This is not something to be taken lightly in a holiday mood, rather, it is for us to give serious consideration to the spiritual freedom given us by our Lord and Savior, Jesus Christ.

Prayer

Heavenly Father, we put our trust in Christ and accept Him as our Lord and Savior. We celebrate life abundant. Just now we commemorate our spiritual independence with bread and cup. Thank You, Lord, for our spiritual freedom. Amen.

—Norman A. Strader
Charleston, Illinois

Date Used: _____

And When He
Had Given Thanks
(Thanksgiving)

Scripture Reading: 1 Corinthians 11:24

(Read Scripture.)

For what did He give thanks, and how was this possible in light of the coming events? He knew full well that in a short time He would be betrayed by one of His own disciples, forsaken by the other eleven, denied by Peter, unjustly tried, falsely accused, and put to a horrible death. Yet He gave thanks.

Does this not teach us a lesson? Whatever life may throw at us, we can still thank God, having the assurance that His all sufficient sustaining grace will see us through.

For what did He give thanks? We are not told. So we can only conjecture. Could it be that He was thankful that now God was bringing to fruition His redemptive system that He had been preparing for centuries?

Or could it be He was thankful that God would sustain Him through these trying times, that even though they would slay Him, He would be raised by God's power?

Whatever the reason, we too can look up and give thanks that we now have an atoning sacrifice for our sins and one who will speak to the Father (1 John 2:1) in our defense, pleading our case before the righteous judge.

Prayer

Our heavenly Father, we thank You for the assurance that Your grace will see us through the trials of this life. We thank You for the example Jesus gave for having an attitude of thankfulness—no matter what trials may present themselves. Thank You just now for this memorial service so we can focus on what Your Son did for us. Amen.

—Paul Berthold
Neoga, Illinois

Date Used: _____

Heart Like a Stable (Christmas)

Scripture Reading: Luke 2:6, 7

(Read Scripture.)

In most homes the month preceding Christmas becomes somewhat hectic, if not frantic. At the very least there are flurries of additional, and sometimes tiring, activities. Shopping, wrapping, sending greeting cards, tree trimming, baking—all blended into a sort of living collage of human activity leading to Christmas Day.

Many of these activities can be seen in Advent calendars, common to European homes. The calendar is a picture into which are cut twenty-four little windows or insets, one for each of the first twenty-four days of December. Behind each window is a symbol of Christmas. It could be a candy cane, a star, an angel, a candle, a gift. One window is opened each day through December 24.

On that day the final pane is opened.

Without fail, there is a small picture of a small babe in a manger, our Savior, Jesus Christ.

There was no room for Him in the inn. He was crowded out. He found refuge in a stable. We do well, during the hubbub of a contemporary Christmas, to slow down and examine our own hearts. Are our lives so crowded that there is no room for Him there? Is He forced out of our lives? Or are our hearts like the stable—warm, ready, and accepting? Let us pray that there is still room there for Him. Where would we be if that twenty-fourth picture were blank, if there were no hope and promise for our lives?

Praise God that Jesus lives!

Prayer

Dear Father, make our hearts warm and accepting like the stable where Jesus was born. Help us to examine our hearts. We pray there is still room for Him. In Your Son's name, Amen.

—William Lainen
McGregor, Minnesota

Date Used: _____

111

Index